Lost Sonnets for My Unvaccinated Lover

Lost Sonnets for My Unvaccinated Lover

Poems by

John Milkereit

© 2023 John Milkereit. All rights reserved.
This material may not be reproduced in any form, published,
reprinted, recorded, performed, broadcast,
rewritten or redistributed without
the explicit permission of John Milkereit.
All such actions are strictly prohibited by law.

Cover image by Kelly Penrod
Cover design by Shay Culligan
Author photo by John Milkereit

ISBN: 978-1-63980-464-1

Kelsay Books
502 South 1040 East, A-119
American Fork, Utah 84003
Kelsaybooks.com

For the gentle lovers

Acknowledgments

I am grateful to the editors of the journals where these poems first appeared.

Abandoned Mine: "[Drifting slowly with you has yet no end]"

The Ekphrastic Review: "[Here's to paddling along]," "[All anyone wants is]," "[Rabbit eats cut lettuce]," "[I went crazy leaping]," "[Cirrus clouds vortex]," "[*Cross my heart*]," "[When a launderette]," "[My lover, lover]," "[My nightmare—fiery dog]," "[The tree is full]," "[If we could paint]," "[Snipped from a garden]"

Kallisto Gaia Press: "[Azaleas rip into bloom]"

Mutabilis Press: "[You write a poem, so you won't]," "[We walk to the art museum]"

Special Thank You

Many of my friends and colleagues contributed to this collection. I'm appreciative of the time and attention given by these individuals and groups:

Poets in the Loop is my monthly critique group where many of these poems were initially workshopped. Thank you, Dom, Winston, Chuck, Mary, Elina, Kelly, Vanessa, Varsha, and Carrie.

David Meischen facilitated several poetry classes online from 2020 to 2022 where I began writing these poems. Several participants read the initial drafts. Tina Carlson, Gabrielle Langley, and Sandi Stromberg read large portions of this manuscript and were instrumental in organizing the poems.

Lorette C. Luzajic, Editor of *The Ekphrastic Review,* kept the bi-weekly challenges coming which I'm forever grateful for.

Toni M. Holland made insightful editorial comments.

Contents

[You write a poem, so you won't]   13
[I breathe in. Then you breathe out]   14
[She models her body]   15
[Rothko Chapel louvers in the ceiling]   16
[Picture your daughter, you, and me]   17
[Every nano transmitter loses sensitivity]   18
[Streaking pills swallowed]   19
[That John Prine song]   20
[I'm a broken barn in Bastrop]   21
[I don't know how romance keeps alive]   22
[Our hands interlace after the long summer]   23
[Your love reminds me of gelato]   24
[James Bond is welded steel]   25
[Horoscope: November 22, 1963]   26
[Drifting slowly with you has yet no end]   27
[Can you touch my voice?]   28
[In early October dusk, a man]   29
[Already, I fly on a carousel of hope]   30
[Sunflower—delicious to the eye]   31
[I guess luck happens]   32
[*All journeys have secret destinations*]   34
[I, as a Cub Scout]   35
[This is a message]   36
[We see and laugh at a man]   37
[I dance to Blippi]   38
[Horoscope for shoes: November 22, 2021]   39
[After teenage fingers finish traveling the keys]   40
[Here's to paddling along]   41
[Serve a blue-belt space for waking]   42
[All anyone wants is]   43
[The next morning, after a cold night]   44
[I drive us home, but]   45
[There is a moment of shopping]   47
[Shopping from home]   48

[Now you pull closer]	50
[I put on silence]	51
[Rabbit eats cut lettuce]	52
[I went crazy leaping]	53
[Cirrus clouds vortex]	54
[Deserted bayou]	55
[We fork breakfast]	56
[Love cannot fill the thickened lung]	57
[Azaleas rip into bloom]	58
[Before, I was your oar man]	59
[Horoscope: November 22, 2023]	61
[*Cross my heart*]	62
[When a launderette]	63
[Dear White Apron,]	64
[Dear Victoria's Secret Lingerie,]	65
[My lover, lover]	66
[I'm a movie theater]	67
[Breathe]	68
[My nightmare—fiery dog]	69
[In the cracked-mirror room]	70
[The tree is full]	71
[Take this totem pole]	72
[When you gurgle as a newborn]	73
[If we could paint]	74
[Snipped from a garden]	75
[We walk to the art museum]	76

You write a poem, so you won't close your eyes.
The poem wants a butterscotch cat patrolling the driveway.

    The cat drives a way into your memory garage.
    My former lover sold enough for a Mary Kay car.

My old love drove her Mary Kay car,
wore nude lipstick and made butterflies from metal sheets.

    Under the sheets, her artful, nude lips fluttered, then said,
    You're the most normal guy I've ever met.

An April day ducks into dusk, normal as TV, no cable,
a nova spotted above a desert.

    On our next date, we spot another nova over a desert.
    We did not say when we would end.

Who has a speech on whether we will end?
You begin to write without closing your eyes.

I breathe in. Then you breathe out and say,

I do not trust the government. July expels its final,

sweet air, dripping away inside a nightclub. I want

luck because I'm not good. Actually, neither.

I am just arteries. Veins. Blood unblocked by calcium.

Leaky thoughts. A mouth sipping on a gin & tonic,

limes cut up, speared. *You might die,* I reply.

I want hopefulness. But, voila! The stage

spotlights a rabbit that causes the magician

to disappear except for his shoes. I exhale.

I want to inject science into some of your DNA.

She models her body up into an array
of light beams and threads a dance.

The window-blind shadows zigzag her face
and cut her torso chasing along a bareness

around her lingerie and polish the dark galaxy
of her waist. Her slow pace could entice a gangster

to forgive murder. A private call dials, a goddess
voice stabs, a virga coming on, a cloud's underside

evaporating as she struts past my dining-room door
that opens to the garage; she is almost giggling,

champagning, smoking her radiant slenderness
near the Queen Anne table where the cherrywood

chairs open the stage for a comet to streak.

Rothko Chapel louvers in the ceiling. August DNA divides the sky.
        Below, purple-black canvas panels meditate.
              You embrace your daughter, Ava, who wears
strawberry-framed glasses. We're on a sand-washed bench

      as if a canoe will tip over in a flashed bayou.

The obelisk outside is broken. Rust-colored pencil point
        on a pyramid. A pool mirrors white clouds, inverted.
        Dragonflies chase in merry-go-round over clipped grass.

I want things back to normal. I study two fallen, grey bird feathers.
        Don't ask me what's in the vaccine. You never asked
                what's in Cheez Whiz.

We try to hold hands under a weeping willow
        streaked with yellow.

Picture your daughter, you, and me as a fallen still shot.

Acorns cling to a twig with leaves on a sidewalk striated.

Grains of cloth. Or birds ready to fly off a cliff into a canyon,

snow dusted along brown and orange rock bands. Until you call.

Out of gas. Robbed earlier. Not sure I have a hundred dollars,

or words left. I buy a red 2.5-gallon gas can. Call her

Rosette, A Can That Cares at Home Depot, aisle 53, and black

nestled funnels, dolls ready to unfasten as whirling dervishes.

I fill up Rosette's body at Valero. Your SUV tank intake doesn't

like any funnel. Not deep enough. Fuel spills, rippling silver waves

outside this sweat-lodge city. We're bad energy. Champagne splits

never help. Now your life wants to gaslight. No, you are your

daughter's best mother. A vaccine tries to speak but is too busy

crying.

Every nano transmitter loses sensitivity when the operator

is Budweiser-induced. When you, Ava, play in the dirt, then you

remind me of the sandbox years. You sketch with a stick

your ballroom dress if your mother will let you go, the excuses

readily available for your mother to mouth *no*—I don't know—

imagination works in a cerulean fog. Every winter day needs

winterization and insulation, and I know, or really feel that now—

when bundled up inside a Honda with a heater cranked to eleven

while trying to fork chunks of tuna from a silvery-pink pouch

and trying to remember if an Easter Lily is your mother's favorite,

not sure, but it's February, and I hope you will go to your ball

and you won't lose your slippers and it's fathomable that Prince

Charming will find you and I know I'm not a prince, and play safe

in your dirt square bordered by sidewalks and a curb while I fill up

your mother's empty tank with gasoline. I wish your bedroom

will have a starry night stuck on the ceiling and a unicorn with

a spiraled, glittery tail will brush the carpet fields, and a doll will

love its push-button that reminds you—sometimes it's necessary,

but not always—to return home before the day darkens.

Streaking pills swallowed
you in the northland. Now on
the gulf coast, bayous
keep buckets reserved to store
your every bright hope trickle.

*

Crack stardusts your ex,
is his heart an asterisk?
His rich daddy wants
you to open a window
to snatch Ava back like a latch.

That John Prine song sings—*hard to believe in this living*.

September ants creep under the windowsill and travel

taupe walls and wrestle in the bathtub. Moses

traveled far, slapping water that turned into blood.

Blood of us. Oxygenated, how much is left, and how far to know

who we really are? We sip our reds, Cabernet and Pinot Noir,

before the next show. The first act at home was seeing

the religion of a hummingbird tracing and retracing a chinaberry

tree. Searching, finding nothing. The vaccine doesn't squash

freedom. You, as unprotected, are the lustrous outline of a legible

health threat. Virus as wilderness. I want us as one country.

If only we could sing, maybe this skeleton key in my pocket

will open our palace door.

I'm a broken barn in Bastrop. You and your beloved
stop to snap pictures of my muffled, red-copper roof.

Fence stakes clasp gun-powder barbed wire.
Once upon a time, the cows prodded their route

into my mouth door and in the morning,
I huffed them out as if cold oxygen. They needed

to chew. Spring is a paintbrush, stroking
the carmine bottle rockets and bluebonnets,

little princes and princesses ready to unlock
their nectars. I cannot eclipse what I was.

I know my shape curves to anchor
my dilapidated, indigo night.

The wind is a pitchfork.
My maker's hammer and nails

will remember me. I understand
if you shutter what is left to touch.

I don't know how romance keeps alive in this jungle.

When I think of you, my favorite thing is raindrops

on raspberries. I claim nostalgia when I see pictures

and negatives hidden in a mismatched sock drawer.

I dream of us on an island now standing in a shuttle

moving slightly above the hard-packed sand, whitecaps

curling, and then collapsing. Sunny afternoon.

We're swaying gently in light-gray smocks holding

onto polished steel bars like on a bus. The virus obliterates

swathes of joy. Hold onto your dream of white-laced lingerie.

We are wandering notes. We are sweating in awkwardness.

When the wind billows around us, we swim a restless sea,

or climb a bubbling volcano or walk a fault line.

Our hands interlace after the long summer

closes. Museum flowers, their small bloom faces,

umbrella relief. Their vibrant white explosions greet

our walk at dusk, faces remnant of used blasting caps.

A possum climbs a tree to spy our dance—

your reasons for not getting jabbed and my rebuttals.

The vaccine was developed too fast, you say.

It's an emergency, I reply. I think of begging her.

Pleading. You nod in promise. In my words, a letter mailed

to the address of a blue-grey cloud ready for beautiful rain.

We unclasp our hands. Without you, I live in a house of furniture.

For dinner, I serve a plate of reservations. The freezer stores

dessert, a sweet carton feeling more and more empty.

Your love reminds me of gelato. Its glittery burst

goes a long way, cooler than a swimming pool's deep end.

The *choco coco* went down to a place where we started.

I want to have what you're having.

A swimming pool goes way down deep, no cooler

than us, the sweet team, whizzing for *oohs & ahs*.

What you're having is better than my have.

The tiramisu left on vacation without proper notice.

The *oohs & ahs* of us whizzing under a dirty set of coconut lights.

We learned from previously dropped scoops. We shovel our

                    gastronomies in pink,

waffling on tiramisu, the flavor floating on a vacation boat.

We'll survive on hyperlocal honey and grass-fed chickens.

Each pink shovel bite is almost better than your taste.

Honey, I'm good to you. I'll scream for you

even if we're running on empty. Cups, empty dreams

won't matter when love bursts, reminding me of gelato.

James Bond is welded steel. I am nicked rubber.

His life is gorgeous and intricate, a sand mandala, blown to wind,

captured and saved. You and I and our broken escalators. This is no

time to die. Dying is our embrace in a capsule of leather seats

at the posh movie theater. We murmur our fantasies. The villain

bullets a sheet of ice to save a blonde. Broken China mask.

Exploding electric eye. Machine guns instead of headlights.

Nano cells ready to launch. Strobed white swords inside a jagged

mountain. In Long-Island-Ice-Tea breath, you exclaim,

It's like Bill Gates infecting us with magnets.

You in a shimmering gold dress with a beige shawl and dental

braces. As if the government wants to track our movement.

No one cares where we are.

                        After the trap door, Bond rescues

his daughter's stuffed monkey. Missiles from friendly ships

complete their faces, their shiny arcs.

Horoscope: November 22, 1963.
JFK's blood formed like a constellation
in a car while you were a moonlit starlet
twinkling in the cosmos. Most humans wind
up better in the outer than the inner world.
Your mother worked at the *Glass House,*
a tollway diner. A walk-up window
for ice cream. Waitresses wore
red and white uniforms and bummed
cigarettes. Do you want to learn how to
swim in the lake or watch the ravens perch,
that Corvid, one rickety letter *r* removed
from another shadow-shifter flight carrying
its message down the throat?
Mating for life is a distinct language.
We enter a jungle, and it doesn't move.
The lake is a breathing body. Learning
water-ballet is another lifeline. Buck
the trend. Break records in your deepish
psychic depths. But remember, you are a fish.
The wind is a messenger. The raven is a bullet.

Drifting slowly with you has yet no end.

You mow the lawn. You don't smoke. You

cover your private parts. You wear a seatbelt so as

not to skid your face across a highway. *No*

freedom no more, you say. Dying has no visitation.

Chemo has no safe wait room. Proust said,

Love is space and time made perceptible to the heart.

Our hours are needles. Our space is stitched where

the thread had been. Ants scurry inside the windowsill

reminding me we have to travel somewhere. I rescue

pinecones in the park for the holidays. I buy squares

of drywall for a home repair only to realize in the parking lot,

a crow waits on my car roof. You aren't near me today,

only the breath of fall collapsing and expanding

as if an accordion begins to play.

Can you touch my voice?
It's a dose that seems foreign.
The fatigue is soft.
Doubts about us are traitors
but sometimes feel like bones, skin.

*

I whisper to you
that we are like two countries
that we want to merge
as one. But I am not sure.
I know dictators that fail.

In early October dusk, a man only wearing pale, tan

shorts, dark crown, belts out gospel in the middle

of West Main Street until he stops and asks: *Are you all*

havin' a good day? Yes, you say. *I have my yogurt*

pouch, see, your daughter voices, soft like a quiet,

gleeful memo. *Do you have the time,* he asks. *6:15 p.m.,*

I reply. *What?* I repeat myself. He threads minutes

and hours through an invisible needle head.

He looks displaced. If we're going somewhere, at least

it's past a white, chipped bathtub. We, the *our-us,*

as in a couple, is washing up. What we need is a little soap.

Water. Wind. Sail. Why not get jabbed for us? Your dark

spirits just whisper because they lost their voices. Let's find

our rhinestone angels. Dragons carry our golden treasure.

This vaccine tango is like shoveling dirt.

Already, I fly on a carousel of hope for you
and your daughter's future. Your faces looking
down or sun-squinted ahead. Milk and honeycomb,
windblown scarves. From there to here, hands
underneath and one is not, for embracing over
a shawl. Sunflowers dressed on wooden horses.
You flourish in hot, dry places. Rich soil.
The "Black Earth." Love is smoke.

I breathe in the looped circus music.
This is a roundabout ride, up and down
(I often feel full of seeing butterflies).

Instead, I stand to admire the circle
of us. My brain says no need to gallop far.
My heart says we have all the oil and seeds.

Sunflower—delicious to the eye, and maybe not

with a bee. A reward for risking a road trip.

You asked and I wanted to. Wanting motion

in my ear, the movement of the Guadalupe River,

the flow of Water Street, locking

memories of a lost job in a junkyard like dogs

behind a fence whimpering for a bone below a rusted

undercarriage.

                      Wanting your daughter to see a giant

teddy bear guarding a floral-shop backdoor. At three,

you say she is blind without her glasses. And wanting

to forget our jailed exes. I wanted the long week

in a small town. Maybe look at lost maples. Forget

your fear of needle-stick. We stuffed our luggage.

We gassed up. We drove west.

I guess luck happens as one sees a ladybug,

spiritual and patient, red shell, black dotted.

Every creature along this river walk is

curious until they're not. See stillness? Lily pads trained

to a sun-exposed eye remember their ancestors,

DNA from another country, living

near a Japanese bridge resisting kayak waves.

A cup-shaped life pollinated by wind, dreaming of nothing,

lime green, blotted inner pink, waiting

for the next four-day bloom party as jewel-toned protectors.

I am suspended, a pastel palette waiting for you to come around.

I am suspended, a pastel palette waiting for you to come around.

For the next four-day bloom party, jewel-toned protectors,

lime green, blotted inner pink, wait.

A cup-shaped life pollinated by wind, dreaming of nothing

near a Japanese bridge resisting kayak waves.

DNA from another country, living

to a sun-exposed eye, remember their ancestors,

curious until they're not. See stillness? Lily pads trained.

Every creature along this river walk is

spiritual and patient, red shell, black dotted.

I guess luck happens as one sees a ladybug.

All journeys have secret destinations of which

the traveler is unaware, something Martin Buber said

to excite you when you've won a tan Ovation guitar

but can't play only to discover your ex-lover could, perched

on her father's torn army cot in a meadow.

                                                  Or a clue

could be the sparrows at Walgreens nesting in the red,

cursive *ess* because you can't stop wondering how to live.

I don't regret this delicate, broken time with you.

May we bloom like white gardenias. May the twigs groan

against windows latched for health and your lungs taste

raindrops dripping on grey planks of the front porch.

Like ducks, we smile at happy hour. Like songwriters, the sets

can't last.

I, as a Cub Scout, could never backward somersault.

I sang "Scarborough Fair" in a grade-school choir. I ice-skated

in Converse High Tops. I built my own town for a model railroad

that meant riding the train downtown to buy trees, a café,

and an Esso gas station where an attendant lifted a nozzle

to fill someone's tank. In 1979, my crush was Aly, who fell in

love with Joc under a wool blanket in the back of the ski-trip bus.

        The leaky crown of my grandfather's watch.

I dreamed of his compass and protractor in a black-snapped

case.

        Today, *Y'all Need Jesus,* says the discarded,

scarlet hat in the garden-center parking lot.

        Who wants to be in need?

Dickinson wrote *Action is redemption.* A snail carries its luggage

near the steps of our cottage inn. I ate gala apples here before.

        Yes, *we have so much to do.* We need our doors,

one for going, and one for the snakes.

This is a message answered or not answered, delivered
    by your ex-lover, inevitable, the end is pain,
        unremarkable as mud in a goat field, the overflow
    parking across Highway 16
from the ranch after the worry and joy of riding night
    through sudden creek back to Quality Inn despite what
        the lux-lit rain gauge read. Still better than before,
Camp Christmas, pitching a tent under mesquite we decorated,
    clipped-on yellow butterflies and hooked cerulean stars.
        Or Camp Question Mark, the banner quilted
from tie-dye shirts and the Frenchy symbol cut from an unwanted
    album sleeve. Now going from one vax question
        to another, each question with a specific face
    like a cat's,
ink-blotted black eyes and fur smelling like an unswept floor,
    orange and the exclamation mark of fall, later turning
        the color of syringes, coats
            holding together answers.

We see and laugh at a man. No, more like a woman

shaped with rock. Hand clutches a boulder purse, one brown

moccasin foot, and a child, like your Ava, with a granite brow,

weather-washed eyes. An Easter Island face teeters

in the background foliage. Along the river, we walk westward,

trekking the slow spiral of our destinies. This year, we find

a new stone labyrinth.

John Cage said, *Get yourself out of whatever cage*

you find yourself in. For us, two cages anywhere.

Don't forget a smaller one for Ava who hand-masks

her mouth when she giggles at today's ducks. She's afraid

of an impoliteness. Soon the path's formal note will end.

The only survivors are cypress trees. We formed as rockscapes.

Rocks heavy inside us.

I dance to Blippi
as a favor to you, Ava,
the musical is cool.
I forget to laugh sometimes
while worry fills my pocket.

*

When I write *pretend,*
there's a rain girl in violet
and yellow inside,
the flower of my younger
self, but my coat weighs a ton.

Horoscope for shoes: November 22, 2021.
Monday—don't worry—your gifts will guide
you home. A Puerto Rican woman,
slender like a daffodil in a white hat who saw
you on display in the back, bottom row
of the store, *Pleasure Zone*. You will ornament
a body. You're a pleaser. Heel to complete
elegant miles. Strutting to eye-ornament.
Your maker ornamented your bottom in rhinestones.
You will mold company at the nightclub. A sliver
of your moon is the hope silver. Two supports
pointing forward, like your owner's eyes ready to
slip into action, as if you're ready to say,
Here I am look at me. And customers will smile
when you turn seamless air that other shoes said
had a bite. You are durable. You can stitch this
breathless world together without complaint.
Press on.

After teenage fingers finish traveling the keys

of a Royal typewriter, the brain sleepwalks

above plaid pajamas under a dark pearl sky.

                                        Salted snow, sidewalk grit,

barefooted, cherry washcloth rests on the bathroom sink edge.

Evidence to show my mother.

Porcelain-tiled bathroom fitted with a cracked mirror,

the only portrait. Bathroom window surveying the wooden stairs.

Balcony of an ice-cream churning area, cranking on ice cubes,

milk, and strawberries after squatting in Michigan in a damp

swimsuit. The grinding contained in a pale-yellow bucket.

                                        So much better now,

the October green land of a small town. You, Ava, and I

a stone's throw from an ice-cream shop fitted inside a yesteryear

rail station. Ava wants chocolate in a sugar cone. Hands to mouths

stuck sweet, dabbing with napkin masks. Ava's scoop topples off

outside in the pebbles. I want to lick a story good enough to go.

Here's to paddling along the shoreline, cypress canopy reflecting on water like painted charcoal. Sun-drunk flies ready for summer glow. Don't worry. You as a mother are a good mother until you forget. A branch doesn't remember how long its life came from a trunk, rings swallowed by dappled foam and yellow fizzle.

Here's a horizon we'll never reach. Here's science dreaming of nothing but calling your name, not a sound, just powder blue air. Here's our moment, a spot along a broken coast, rippling, ready to rub away. Our existence folds in Earth's pocket of an oilskin jacket. Here's to the religion of our boat coming on without mistake, whispering for you to wake.

Serve a blue-belt space for waking.
The buckle is a bridge for your boat
to navigate toward a paradise shore,
but what if, on the other side,
there are Antarctica tears? Instead,
pretend to write a poem from fiction.
Or look at a photograph of an iceberg
with your lover. A magic trick holds
the body still. Each exposure, every
minute centers breath. Today,
your planet is Mercury. Water
rusts the isolated terrain yet grows
one earthly branch and heavenly stem.

One earthly branch and heavenly stem
grows the isolated terrain yet rusts
your planet, Mercury. Water, minute
by minute, centers breath. Today,
still the body. Each exposure, every
magic trick holds your lover
with an iceberg photograph, or look
at a poem as fiction. Pretend to write
a *there,* about Antarctica tears instead.
But what if, on the other side,
you navigate toward a paradise shore
where the buckle is a bridge for your boat?
Serve a blue-belt space for dreaming.

All anyone wants is a clean, bathed

sky in pink notes. I'm hovering

over a snowy roof. Paris, *je t'aime.*

The Ghost of Future lifts me via sleigh.

My ice bones and half-stabbed, frozen lungs.

Feet groan to land. Roof of innocence.

Roof of chalky slate. I can't open your shuttered

windows. I can't climb down your chic facade.

Our reality has run adrift so let's start

anew on a white blanket. Spring is a promise to us

living in a cherry blossom frame sipping cognac

and amaretto in a courtyard. The glow of this scene

awakens. *S'il vous plait,* I gulp each breath

in night neon.

The next morning, after a cold night, the condensate

invites Ava to finger-draw on a water-beaded windowpane.

In the thickest streak, she says, *the roof of our tiny house.*

A steep pitch like an arrow remains and dapples off. What

was once a frame dribbles down and other droplets connect

windows and a door. Her index fingernail taps in exclamation

for a knob.

Look. Here, you will live with us. Human shapes

smudge. My torso is the imprint from yesterday's bird collision.

It's hard to see us; pretend. Flecks of mud mismatch

as shoes above the caulked, smooth molding.

She pauses to push her eyeglasses up her nose. Pupils

telescope in clairvoyance. *Yes, I know, that's the backyard.*

A clear, gold-green necklace of trees. Above the window latch is

a curtain for a cloud-plumped sky.

This is our last cottage day. I stuff our luggage.

I drive the car and then remember I forgot to sweep the floor.

I drive us home, but the steering wheel judders.
The white-striped, cracked highway clasps
pleasure, jog of a memorable trip. I remember your tears
on the white comforter and trying to diagnose
the dry sighs of your mother's variant
attitude on your jabless status. She is bold,

says *no* to your visits. The spinach lasagnas in foil-folded
pans as drop-off gestures. Kitchen appliances juddering.
Now tumbleweeds of silence roll. Someone is packing our variant
lives in freight cars. These billboards clasp
sharp edges and our vision. I exit for gas, die, who knows
for a better romantic story, a body of lines with periods of tears.

We pocketknife initials in a picnic table. Tears
in paper napkins. Tuna-salad sandwiches wrapped boldly,
taped cellophane. Millions of minutes left for lunching, diagnosing
the route. The odometer counts the remainder and our muttered
breaths. Marriage is not something to plug into like grabbing
an electric cord for a socket. We see hook-ups of busted variation

for campers before we toss our leavings. I want a variant
vision of normal. Boredom tears.
I outstretch arms and clasp
my hands around your waist, look ahead, echoes of a bold
undertaking. Hope tracks. Railroad crossing arms judder
in wind off the feeder. I-10 also speaks, a dial

for high blood pressure. Without a code, we drink to diagnose
our gears—this direction, tooth by tooth, variable
happiness. You can't buy love but at least you can judder
away a rescue act. You can't steal love like tearing
souvenirs from spindly racks: maps, postcards, a bold-
trimmed Western hat. Long, lanky telephone lines grasp

poles above gravel roads. Entrance gates gasp
at ranches in chained loops. Stopping at a rest area, we diagnose
the quiet autumn leaves scattered in sunlit bands. Gold
water streams from a fountain. Variant
bird swallow. We unrest our hollow bottles and tear,
no, unscrew lids to fill up. Bodies ready to steer despite juddering.

For every mile marker, bold clock hands clasp.
Our murky insides flutter. We diagram
a variant future that could go kablooey, where everything tears.

This is a moment of shopping inside a temporary retail space.

This is an October riveted with stars. You as Harley Quinn.

A moment of masks, green-striped pumpkins, boxed costumes hatched from cellophane windows and cardboard.

To makeup dialed in midnight color. Only heaven knows where it's applied.

This is a moment down Richmond Avenue at La Tapatia. Park across the street. Margaritas flowing, skinny flute stems, tequila with 100% agave nectar. Standard.

This is the moment absorbed into sweet.

This is a TV on mute, a soccer match in faded pixels.

This is a moment drifting . . . you and me and a place of want.
      Stone streets, mariachis, local chocolate bar
           broken and the sound of a whirling blender.

This is a moment inside our *posada*. Rooms converted from the *monjas*.
      Cracked window.
    Backyard with a roped tire ready to swing from a branch.

The moment of awakening. Rooster crow.

Shopping from home. Clicking images,
all the foods I once loved to touch.

The personal shopper better select
avocados I approve of. Not mushy,

not ripe, yearlings ready for a new climate.
There's no carrot to click for less than

1 lb. of red seedless grapes, too much
for a family of one. Love buying popcorn,

kernels bathed in movie-theater butter,
pop into a dome, slit roof. Steam soft hissing out.

Personal shopper, I'm on schedule, here now,
texting my arrival spot, F630.

I see in the rearview mirror how I saw you
before—petite, masked mystery mouth,

gripping plastic bag handles. Trunk lever pulled.
Then you stun me, tapping on the window glass

I lower. *Sir—do you want the eggs upfront with you?*
as if driving is too hazardous

for the little organic darlings. *Yes, I guess so,*
I say, wanting to see your fingers,

grabbing the bag, my fingers touching,
grazing yours, a subtle invitation.

Hopeful to see your blue irises deep
like an oasis. Closer to drink you in.

Each sip of juice, if not seedless, pulped foreplay.
We could eat packaged migas

and nestle in the back seat. Car heat on,
sunroof open, snow dusting the yellow-striped lanes.

Now you pull closer and move into *Susanne,*
the apartment complex across the street
from the grocery store with curbside delivery.

River oaks saved, branches weave
the parking lot. A building constructed over
torn down, condemned dwellings with empty

Coke cans tinkled in pebbles while cocaine bags
stood rooted and passed between rattlesnake hands.
Tonight, you and Ava, pull closer as stars might,

thick and wild dandelions, edging across a luminous
sky. Night clouds have broken apart so you both
whisk as a kind of dizziness in whirling gray air.

I imagine pushing Ava in a bigger cart. She would
touch the avocadoes. Your fingers would tap
a champagne bottle and your lips would purse open

on small, expensive cheeses and fragile crackers.
Oh, *Susanne,* please take care of my loves despite
your recent gas leaks.

Plato said: *Be kind, for everyone you meet is engaged in
a difficult struggle.* Oh *Susanne,* I will try to gentle myself.
I will try to forget that dawn will deliver as cold and still.

I put on silence
except when I zip dress pants.
While I'm still alive,
how does breath chase the living,
how does breath button a shirt?

*

Dear lover, lover
I want to hear your voice now.
Sometimes what you say
brings a waking like orchids,
sometimes the night rain ballets.

Rabbit eats cut lettuce
like the way spruce cut up
the pale silk heaven

Hold still
the grass where I stand out

Another rabbit waits
like the way the afternoon castles me

White-gate mouth shuts
the marigold road

I walk into fortune's mouth
buttoned to return as the boy
not to lose the lettuce

I want to feed again
tomorrow and tomorrow

I want to come closer to you

Rabbit doesn't eat cut lettuce
Behind the tower window
I'm on the lookout waiting

I went crazy leaping to your shoreline
beneath the Pleiades—those seven sisters,

and the lunar crescent, the blue-green-midnight
film, your mother's voice, late spring wrapped

in a beach blanket lodged in dunes. Here your origin
began beaded as a necklace of time

when tide was the most moon stricken, rainbows,
sun boats, bodies far in the cosmos yet close enough,

breathing zones rising and setting, sketching
a shadow-pitched perimeter. Measure the earthwork.

I'll go crazy if I don't go crazy for your future
treasure pit. I can't promise bronze swords, hatchets,

chisels, or spiral bracelets. I'll start your memory plate
and oars to navigate, flower gloss, and the illuminated

sheen from your gold orbs. Your surface will grow
as beautiful as your aura, conceived as thick, still stars

watched from a clear sky while your mother's nails
drew enough blood to lick for a blessing.

Your heavens will sew and synchronize like fields.
The rhythm is sand dollars, broken by current.

Cirrus clouds vortex,
red-flecked wings, and water
foam-like small bodies,
the current momentous. Sand
pricks my skin like needles.
I wait to see what is more
viscous. Gulf coast birds
point like poured milk.
My new soul will be a song.

A room of framed waves.
My voice bleaches in day blue.
I love a mouth in quiet white.

Deserted bayou
where secrets submerge under
a bridge that masks your anger.
Revenge is a note, pushed
away, faithless, fury so
focused on precious stones
not for another woman.

Love has more than one vowel.
Vengeance draws down a deep well,
sinking city where
I want soap, not soap operas.
Theater flames will not burn the
ink of my last consonant.

We fork breakfast sitting on bar stools. I remember
the flesh-colored marble counter and the Bloody Marys
we could not order. No alcohol before 7 a.m.
We drink coffee spiked, heavy pour from our flasks.

The flesh-colored marble counter and the Bloody Marys
I knew would lead to a nervous moment:
us drunk from spiked coffee
smoothing course edges just as

I knew this would lead to a nervous moment.
As a couple, our first masked flight
smoothing course edges,
kissing you under dim yellow lamplight,

yet us as a couple, our first masked flight,
steams up the airplane bathroom—rough unzipping,
kissing you close to a small white bulb.
Crazy how love ricochets in tight quarters.

The steamed-up bathroom, the unzipping. Rough.
I remember forking breakfast and sitting on bar stools.
I'm quartered crazy. Love ricochets
without alcohol before 7 a.m. What is *order?*

Love cannot fill the thickened lung with breath.

I know my veins overfill with her existence.

The unfiltered glow of the Galleria is a flavor

where I haul the bags. Her truth and reality fulfilled

by a gold chain, the Gucci calfskin purse, lungs filling

up after meeting the devil named Phillip, who sold

her Fendi tennis shoes, low-topped, filled fashion where

I ask how God's breath fills up and fogs a glass counter

after that transaction. When I fulfill my honey-do list,

she whispers for slices of honeydew to fill a little

copper-glazed bowl to eat over our cotton-filled

bedspread. Later, perhaps fish filleted at the Palm

for dinner to refill her scent of the sea.

Her unconvinced heart races, her favorite filly possibly.

Note: The first line is from Edna St. Vincent Millay's poem, "Love is Not All (Sonnet XXX)."

Azaleas rip into bloom after the throat
of winter quiets to a whisper.

Stop waltzing around the patio
waving crinkled sage. Chalked hearts

beat on a sidewalk. Yellow-headed night herons
decorate with white excrement,

confetti jumping on dots of bricks and leaves
for a homecoming you aren't invited to.

When she offers you pineapple juice
and Southern Comfort in her dead father's glass,

go ahead. Drink. This is the cream of the crop—
flowers pour gently their thick nectar. A heron calls

maw-maw, maw-maw under a live oak canopy.
This is the trampoline season. When the super pink

moon burns through a dark curtain, its beads of light,
rising and falling, will awaken you.

Before, I was your oar man trying to get us past this furious

foam drawn back like a dark curtain. Whip of wind

blew dry strands of hair in your mouth. Nothing

magical to see.

                    I'm not a magician wanting to saw women

in half or hold a dove. Now I rise, in the middle of an airport,

after reading about pygmy rabbits, whiskers away

from extinction. Sagebrush survivors land their shots.

I pee in the dim light of the bathroom. Andy Williams

pipes in from speakers singing . . . *A great big bundle of joy*

when he's coming down the chimney.

                          The little girl back in the seating area

tries to lift her bigger sister. Fun and games, hands interlocked

around the waist, while we wait for the late plane. Each wear

a matching glittered mask. The rise and fall.

                                  We visited my retired

parents so they could meet you. We played cards until the spots rubbed off. We ate blistered carrots and orange-kissed mahi-mahi. Elvis arises . . . *Hear the snow crush, see the kids bunch . . . you hear silver bells.* I remember his billiard table with the cue stick tearing the greenery.

        The lush green landscape of us. The worry streaks.

Horoscope: November 22, 2023.
Time to break open and hear a Wednesday
seagull call. A kind of escape.
You're born today. The unfiltered breaths
begin already. Architecture for passion,
magnetized for mystery. Earth surf scorched
smooth. Palmettoes, black silhouettes,
defiant and bare. I sit in the waiting room
and think of a pocket, stitched shape, and handiness.
All the usefulness, as a place of storage.
Your openness to positive shifts.
Your reel from the chaos you will have to
witness. Nothing about a kite
is without purpose. No brain,
not knowing where the shoreline is.
Birth is a cradle of hands.

Cross my heart and hope to die,

I murmured at eleven years old during Spin the Bottle.

That game's amber beer bottle spun and stopped,

open-mouthed neck said to kiss a strange girl.

Her hands were like winter ghosts. Her wrists skirted

with gray and white crosshatched cloth, ruby ends,

pearl buttons and midnight blue thread.

Unfolding from squatting positions, we merged

so everyone would stop laughing. Lather of cold paste

on my forehead. When our lips met, slick moisture.

We swam in flashed light to a deep pool.

Today, she is a blonde grownup.

Her eye is stuck on babies and I'm a spinning bottle.

The man she wants is a shadow fantasy. All I want is

to sip an everlasting elixir to survive this porous, precious life—

no basement, no laughter,

no snowbound December night.

When a launderette
smokes its billowing breath, I
think of December's
grin and after cardinals
swoop to love the thin
branches of a birch duet,
we bundle with gloves,
our dreams and days astonished.
When they leave, they ink our minds.

Snow is now a mask.
I want to cover my face.
The red runs raw of
our daily news. Straight rungs on
a ladder will rescue us.

Dear White Apron,

You wrap around my mother's waist, like an umbilical cord,
during her latest kitchen concoctions. The wrought-iron bars cover
windows reminding me of mascara. You cover my dietitian mother
who cooks while advising grocery-store shoppers.

We're the newfangled test children for her *Runner's Cookbook*.
We turn away from wheat germ and raisin cookies.

What happens to children who want to survive on pickles
and chocolate milk? And when my father prank-calls my mother
about a runover turkey squashed pale in the parking lot?

Whatever happens inside the kitchen drawer stored with thin,
white envelopes, and penciled titles like *Food, Power, Lunch $$$?*
The record player grooved, "Take Me Home, Country Roads."
I don't remember the rest of the lyrics.

I shovel snow quilted on the neighbor's sidewalk and stairwells,
shoveling enough inches to earn enough to buy packets of baseball
cards and pink gum coarse as a cat's tongue. Tiny compartments.
Everything stays in its lanes. Fragile borders.

White apron, looking back, you were practical, translating yourself
to serve and protect. We don't marry our mothers. Then your
lingerie cousin came along, that Victoria's Secret skin, lace
plunging my unvaccinated lover. Urges reflect on mirrors dreamt
overhead, inverted, and what can we harness from our hackneyed
carousel, awkward smiles open to ride on and on as far as we can.

Dear Victoria's Secret Lingerie,

An ocean of time before we meet at an Indian restaurant, my lover and I merge unexpectedly at your front door. She's in rose-flushed shock. She waves a coupon, wanting you as an umbilical cord to wrap around her Madonna waist.

We stroll through your garden after a pause, leaving complicated breaths. The brunette in a poster is sporting you, a contorted flamingo. Her teeth-whitened smile melts the Christmas tree behind her.

Perhaps my lover will select you as a Snake Charmer Teddy, Strawberry Corset Crop Top, or Satin-Jacquard Open-Back Romper? It's difficult to say what she will pick. The quiet whispers over bedroom threads.

You're an accomplice. This pursuit is drunk with lust, no mother marriage.

At the restaurant, desire dances over a plain, white tablecloth. We swallow large gulps of ice water. We share a chai tea.

We eat curry and garlic naan. The memory of a white apron is a vapor cloud.

My lover, lover,
there are feathers above my head.
My eye is open
and my unmasked face wants you
but half is shaded.

*

When I paint violet,
the canvas is a winter angel.
The hopeful couples
have never seen dreams my way,
have never seen snowflake wings.

I'm a movie theater, a forest of lush chairs
and reclining, leather seats, paired
in love-dome shells for date night.
On the horizon, I see you order teriyaki chicken
on skewers and a Long Island Iced Tea.
I'm a hired lens. I see nothing to reflect
the patrons' aloneness away from home.
They come again and murmur, giggle, and empty seats
shaped as silhouettes of absent souls wanting
this escape, escaping normal day-shadow.
I'm aware, yes. I do see and project.
The patrons' schedule is to suspend and widen
and forget but I'm not a memory-keeper.
I'm a story, percolating from a pewter screen,
stories regardless of any or no vaccine,
your story when you unmask my story
after the curtains close.

Breathe.

Breathe in.

Breathe without stopping.

My nightmare—fiery
dog, a pale horse, and a grey wolf
licking their last licks
on a sprawling trunk at dusk.
Terror begins when they
see my naked, thin figure,
a body Giacometti
might have bronze-casted for a
promised-green turf. Life's lost tongue.

The vagabond face
between the robed spirit's
legs masks a warning. I want
a breath to find my
clothes. Rope tugs from the mouth, oh
that animal-stupid want!

In the cracked-mirror room, we steer,
quick and slow on the salsa floor—hole

inside my stomach—and, nectar,
inhale your blood orange, blonde leather,

and white woods. Demons appear behind
in dizziness, bronze winged, curled tails, burnt

tongue-laughter, taunting my 2-3-5 & 8 roll
while they squash other chickened students.

The recess-lit habitat has a yield strength of
taffeta: I bite the minutes, roll a mouthful,

press your lovely shoulder blade the way I want
love pressed into. Right left right and scariness

or spaghetti awkwardness. Happiness is a horned
god that centers the body. I am a nomad fighting

past every past & future variant of myself.
I'm concerned about the unbitten

Fredericksburg peaches and the hatch green
chiles from our last road trip—another salsa

recipe to ruin. Try to enjoy the dance without
beads of sweat. Trust that a *titanic* array,

a shimmering zenith will lead with steps to follow.

The tree is full of undisturbed mystery

against an egg-fed sky. The tree is full,

nature's way does not lick as much as blanket,

olive knots swath around the trunk.

It's September. Life is seeping from seed

and skin. Branches quiver, fingers ready to touch

a bird's breath. Of chiseled blueness,

our baby will taste the wind zinging

like a Copper Canyon Train. Jump on,

ride through Shangri-La-like valleys

of cool alpines, and you see a conductor

reading *Don Quixote,* now a horse like Rocinante,

now wake off an epic dream swept as cloudless,

and now smell mountain marigolds outside

the lowered windows, dusk smells of citrus,

and now a horizon cracks open, poached.

Take this totem pole and the carved top
of a thunderbird face. This kind of hollow column
where my mouth should have been. You murmur
wildman of the woods before we drive off, a couple
working on friction. Take these hands to rub. Drive
for a doctor's appointment. Our cub sounds stronger.
I've got a spirit bear inside myself as if I'm a zoologist,
but I'm not. We work on us, a matching set,
yet my hands won't quite interlace yours.
This kind of column murmurs hardware
of a carved wisdom. A sea wails against our shores.
Waves curl and curling, crest flecks into
our composition. The body wants to rush, rush.
It's like I'm rescuing and escaping you.
The way this drive is. My feet don't always pedal.
My hands wish they were eagles. Columns stand
brilliantly in the park. Animals know their position.
The sea is an emerald face. The shore is more
like a red cedar door. This kind of wildman carved
for sky and thunder ready for nothing,
nothing left to take away.

When you gurgle as a newborn, then you grow.

We swaddle our baby in a blanket like this aura

of color *to slow the circles down*

as Joni Mitchell sang. Perfect circles, child

as a new white arc that finds a white spiral

and grows up as the boy who trades his feather

collection for a handful of magic coffee beans

and tea bags to plant—a beaming canvas plot—

shooting a light-green stalk bolting past

orange leaves and a buttered sky. I'll buy

my son binoculars for his voyage to steer

clear of icebergs ahead unlike the Titanic crew

who never had the key to unlock the binocular

locker and every bay of marine blue is clear water but

tender truth and one truth is he'll shed his skin,

hair, shells, horns, and other layers he owns—

ink for the gentle, giant melody, *round*

and round in the circle game of timeless molt.

If we could paint time, let's brush with minimal gloss.
See, we don't want tongues as daggers.

If speech were shaded grey and blue-black,
let's not speak until the blasted surfaces clear,

diamond-shaped tears dry, mouths ready for a republic.
Listen, disinformation is the wreckage of a burned-out star,

sunlight, the disinfectant I've been trying to offer.
If a shot had a chocolate cake factor,

divide medicine looking good divided by goodness
= *wellness* or when the torn newsprint

of science is worn as chain mail while our innocent
bodies blush against the air, say in *Guernica,* our eyes

will spy doves, screaming for peace, couples, tolerant,
magnetic aerial shows. What if a bull appeared

from a horse's bent leg like magic, your hands would slip
into pockets of rain smelling clove-like with carnations.

If we escape this smoke and these cracks don't break us,
fields will rejoice, drawn in lavender, almond trees

will awaken, buttoned white coats.

Snipped from a garden, roses breeze the room.
They live urned near a stone ledge.

Adulthood is sledding the snow-sculpted hill
in the park until the bottom. The past acts

like a ghost crawling from a fireplace no one cleaned.
What keeps returning is the strange navy glow

of a Cub Scout shirt and shock of the first coat and tie
lying on a bed to wear for grandfather's funeral.

The future is chained to the past—now ashes.
Adulthood is not a fair exchange and one way

of staying alive is to avoid a stone ledge
while sleeping with red poppies and to remember

the soul looks like other souls walking a gaslit street.
Another way to rise above the topsoil is to stop

counting the remaining days like morning glories,
their tender seeds once buried in pots.

Today, the pharmacist is a goddess in her white jacket,
eyes flowered dark. She inserts the needle.

We walk to the art museum before it closes and then we walk

in the tunnel under domed blue, green, and peppery orange lights

to the café. I know you would like more babies and no matter if

it's your second marriage, I'm happy as a father. The situation

clumps into an ephemeral intimacy with ice cream cups like

O'Keeffe's white flowers on canvas. We're not unusual.

We're like flowers. We stay rooted in one coordinate,

yearning for unfiltered breath, hoping something good happens

with light and shade. We're planted on purpose. Yes, different

stems and different earth origins, but we're still flowers riddled

and flushed on a cold, January edge guarded by bronze statues,

outside here before us, that will outlast us.

About the Author

John Milkereit moved to Houston, Texas from Atlanta, Georgia in 1991 and currently works as a mechanical engineer. He grew up in Chicago in the 1970s where he was first introduced to poetry by having to read "Beowulf" in the sixth grade. He did not return to poetry until 2005 when his local minister began conducting poetry seminars.

He has since been published in various literary journals including *The Comstock Review, Naugatuck River Review, San Pedro River Review,* and *The Ekphrastic Review*. He has attended various poetry conferences such as San Miguel Poetry Week, Colrain Manuscript Conference, and the Pt. Townsend Writing Conference. He also has been a featured reader at various events such as *First Friday, Houston Poetry Fest,* and the Sundown Poetry Series as part of Piccolo Spoleto in Charleston, South Carolina. He also served as judge for various poetry events and served on the board of Mutabilis Press, a non-profit press dedicated to publishing poetry. He has also been nominated for a Pushcart Prize.

He completed a B.S.M.E. at Georgia Tech in 1988. He completed a low-residency M.F.A. in Creative Writing at the Rainier Writing Workshop in 2016. He has published two chapbooks (Pudding House Press) and three full-length collections of poems, including from December 2022, *A Place Comfortable with Fire* (Lamar University Literary Press).

He experienced a mild case of COVID-19 before a vaccine was available. The characters presented in these poems are figments of his imagination.

www.ingramcontent.com/pod-product-compliance
Lightning Source LLC
Chambersburg PA
CBHW031203160426
43193CB00008B/491